W9-BLO-683

Colosseum in Rome

ANCIENT · ROME ·

DANIEL COHEN

ILLUSTRATED BY

HIGGINS BOND

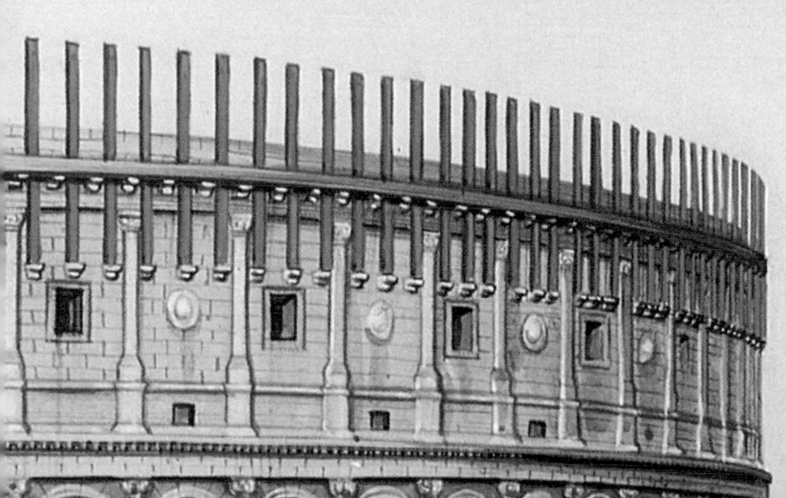

A DOUBLEDAY BOOK FOR YOUNG READERS

Books in this series:

The Amish by Doris Faber
Ancient Egypt by Daniel Cohen
Ancient Greece by Daniel Cohen
Ancient Rome by Daniel Cohen
Apes and Monkeys by Donald R. Shire
Cars by George Sullivan
Dinosaurs by Daniel Cohen
Exotic Birds by Marilyn Singer
How Life Began by Melvin Berger
The Human Body by Gilda Berger
Insects and Spiders by Lorus J. and Margery Milne
Jungles by Mark Rauzon
Mathematics by Irving Adler
Prehistoric Animals by Daniel Cohen
Prehistoric People by Bruce Coville
Reptiles and Amphibians by Howard E. Smith
Seasons by Melvin Berger
Sharks by Gilda Berger
Stars and Planets by Christopher Lampton
Weather by Howard E. Smith
Whales by Gilda Berger
Zoos by Daniel and Susan Cohen

Special thanks to Dr. Robert Steven Bianchi of the Brooklyn Museum for his careful review of the manuscript and illustrations.

A Doubleday Book for Young Readers
Published by Delacorte Press
Bantam Doubleday Dell
Publishing Group, Inc.
666 Fifth Avenue,
New York, New York 10103
Doubleday
and the portrayal of an anchor with a dolphin are trademarks of Bantam Doubleday Dell Publishing Group, Inc.
Library of Congress Cataloging-in-Publication Data
Cohen, Daniel
Ancient Rome / Daniel Cohen; illustrated by Higgins Bond.—1st ed.
p. cm.
Summary: A thorough introduction to history, major figures, and events that shaped Rome.
Includes index.
1. Rome—History—Juvenile literature. [1. Rome—History.]
I. Bond, Higgins, ill. II. Title.
DG209.C63 1992
937—dc20 90-14101 CIP AC
ISBN 0-385-26066-0
RL: 3.7

Manufactured in U.S.A.
September 1992
10 9 8 7 6 5 4 3 2 1 RMC

Children of the Wolf

Two thousand years ago, Rome was the most powerful city in the Western world. Visitors came to see its great buildings and monuments. They were often taken to the center of the city and shown a tiny and ancient round hut that had been carefully preserved near the emperor's palace.

This, the visitors were told, was where it all began. This was the hut of Romulus (ROM-u-lus), the founder of Rome.

The Romans told many different stories or myths about how their city began. The most popular was about the twins Romulus and Remus (RE-mus). They were the sons of the war god Mars. As babies, their mother put them in a basket and set it afloat in the Tiber (TIE-bur) River.

The basket came to rest under a fig tree in front of a cave. A she-wolf took care of the twins. Later they were found and adopted by a shepherd and his wife.

When they grew to manhood the twins decided to found a city. But they fought about boundaries, and Romulus killed Remus. He then went on to become the first king of Rome. The name Romulus means "man of Rome."

During the days of Rome's glory, the Romans thought about the rise of Romulus from abandoned baby to founder of a great city. Later when Rome was torn by civil wars, setting Roman against Roman, they remembered the other part of the myth —how Romulus killed his brother.

Alps
Austria
Switzerland
Yugoslavia
Gulf of Venice
Adriatic Sea
France
Arno River
ITALY
Corsica
Tiber River
Rome
Ionian Sea
Palermo
Sicily
Mediterranean Sea

Who the Romans Were

Today Rome is no longer the center of the Western world. It is still a great city, the capital of modern Italy. Italy itself is a boot-shaped country jutting into the Mediterranean Sea from the southern edge of the continent of Europe. It is separated from the rest of Europe by the Alps mountains. Rome is located near the mouth of the Tiber River about halfway down Italy.

Many people thought the city of Rome was founded on seven hills in the year 753 B.C. While there had been villages in the area long before 753 B.C., they did not get together to form a city until many years later. No one is sure exactly when.

The people who lived in this area were sturdy, hardworking farmers and herdsmen. For these early Romans the family was the center of life, and the father was absolute head of the family. Their religion was simple and practical. The family carried out certain rituals for the gods. This, they believed, pleased the gods, who in return helped the crops grow and allowed the family to prosper.

The life of these people was not very different from that of hundreds of other small settlements throughout Italy. Gradually the various settlements around the mouth of the Tiber got together to form the city of Rome.

Rome prospered in a modest way. But it remained backward, certainly nothing like the great cities of Greece, Egypt, Persia, or other parts of the Mediterranean and Middle East.

the god Apollo

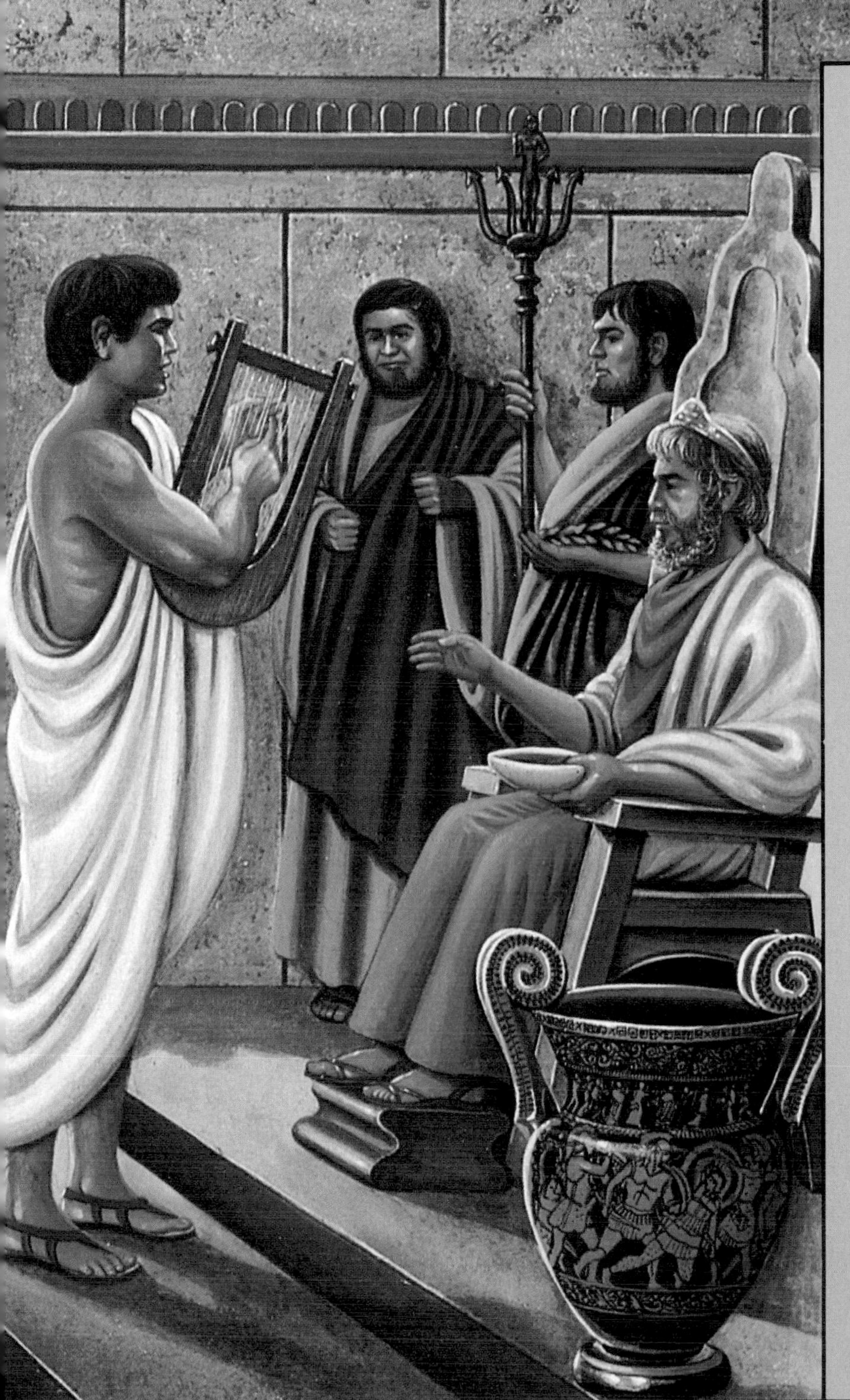

The Etruscans

During the time that the city of Rome was just getting started, large parts of Italy were controlled by the Etruscans (E-trusk-ans).

The Etruscans were more advanced than the people of early Rome. They lived in well-developed city-states—though the Etruscan city-states were always at war with one another. The Etruscans were architects, artists, merchants, and soldiers. They spoke a language that was quite different from any other known language. Even today, the few written works they left behind are not fully understood.

Rome fell under the influence of the Etruscans. For well over a century Rome was ruled by Etruscan kings. Ultimately the Romans came to resent them, and around 510 B.C. the last of the Etruscan kings was driven out of Rome.

Yet the Etruscan kings had done a lot for Rome. The city was larger, richer, and more powerful than before. The Etruscans themselves didn't disappear. Many remained in Rome and mixed with the general population. But the power of the Etruscan kings over Rome was broken forever.

The Republic

The revolt that drove out the last Etruscan king was led by wealthy families, the aristocrats of Rome. These families decided that they had had enough of kings. So they established the Roman Republic.

The political power in the Republic rested with the Senate, a body of men from the aristocratic families. There was also an Assembly of all Roman citizens, but it didn't have much power. A variety of elected and appointed officials did the day-to-day work of running the city. The most important of these were the *consuls.* The consuls had great authority, but there were strict limits. They were elected for a term of only one year, and there were

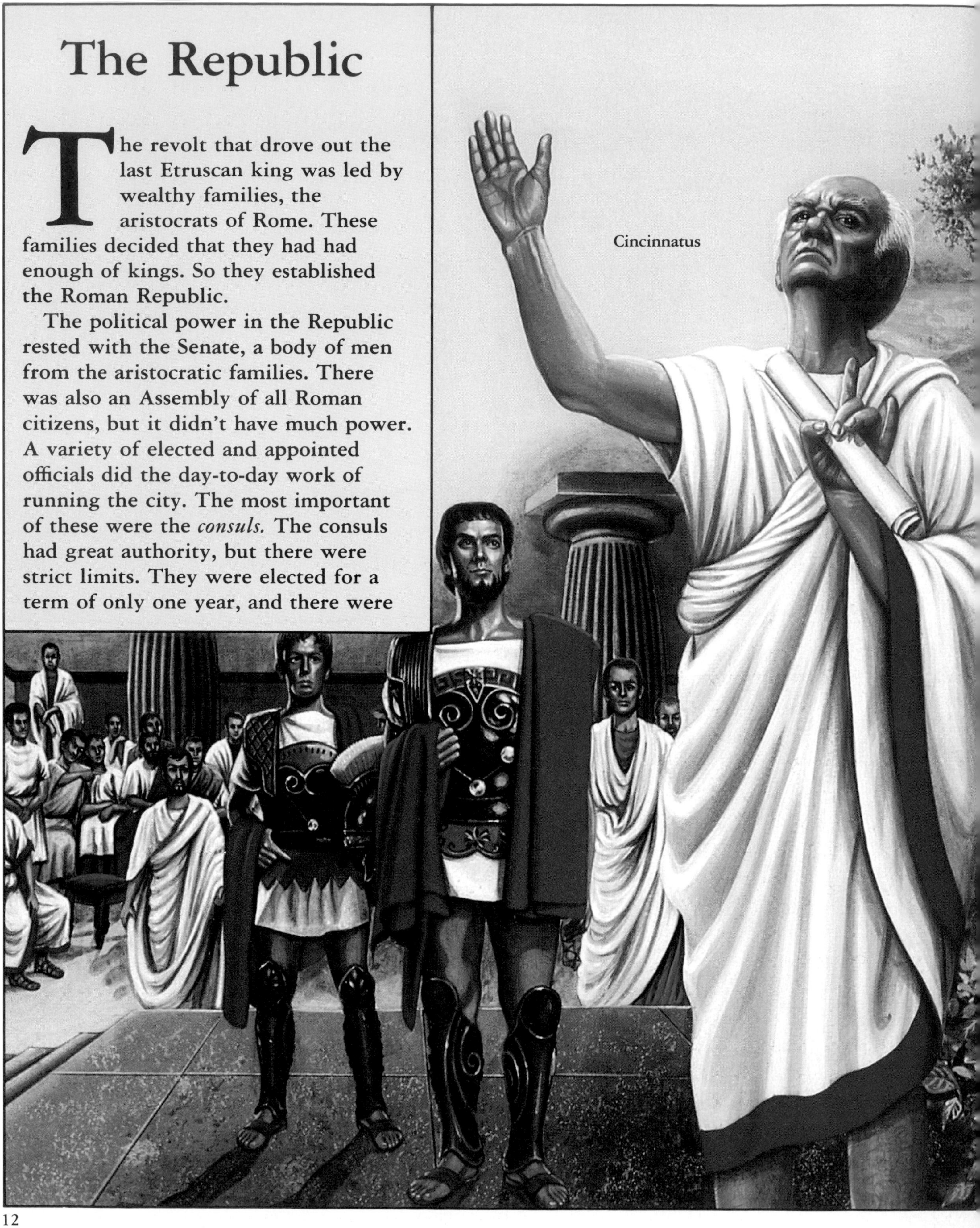

Cincinnatus

always two consuls. One could not act without the approval of the other. The Senate wanted to be sure that no single man would become too powerful.

In times of extreme emergency a single leader called a *dictator* could be appointed. He was to serve for six months or less. The ideal dictator, indeed the ideal Roman, was a man called Cincinnatus (Sin-si-NAT-us).

Like most Romans of the early Republic, Cincinnatus was a farmer. Around the year 458 B.C. a Roman army was trapped by fierce mountain tribesmen. The Senate sent a messenger to Cincinnatus to tell him he had been appointed dictator to deal with the crisis. The messenger found him at work in his fields.

Cincinnatus immediately put down his plow and picked up his sword. He took command of a relief force and in two weeks had rescued the army. Then he resigned and went back to working his fields.

Cincinnatus was held up as the perfect example of all the old Roman virtues. He was a simple, hardworking farmer, a fine soldier, and a man who did not want personal glory, whose only desire was to serve Rome.

Rome and Her Enemies

Slowly, but very surely, Rome began conquering neighboring cities. By 264 B.C. Rome controlled most of Italy.

Conquest is only half the story. The Romans were also clever politicians and excellent administrators. Rome was able to manage the lands it conquered.

As Rome became more powerful it went to war with another power in the Mediterranean, the city of Carthage (CAR-thedge). Carthage was located on the coast of North Africa, but had colonies all over the Mediterranean and a powerful fleet. The two cities first went to war in 264 B.C., and after twenty-three years Rome was victorious. But Carthage was able to

rebuild and in 218 B.C. again challenged Rome, this time with a leader of genius.

His name was Hannibal (HAN-ah-bul). He led his army out of Carthaginian colonies in Spain, traveling over the Alps and into Italy.

Perhaps Hannibal's name would be less famous today if not for the thirty-seven unusual members of his army—elephants. Actually, most of the elephants died crossing the Alps. Those that remained were not very good in battle. But Hannibal didn't need elephants. By his military skill he very nearly brought Rome to its knees. His army ravaged Italy for seventeen years, until finally he was forced to give up the war.

Historians consider Hannibal one of the greatest generals of all time. He lost because he had underestimated the loyalty Rome inspired in other parts of Italy. Hannibal expected that after a few victories, those lands that Rome had conquered would come over to his side. Some did, but most remained with Rome. So in the end it was Rome's political skill, not her army, that really defeated Hannibal.

The Rise of the Generals

The general Gaius Marius (GUY-us MAR-e-us) changed the nature of the Roman army. Before him, the army had been made up of citizen soldiers who owned land. Like Cincinnatus they could go back to their farms after the war was over. But Marius recruited his army from among the landless poor. He trained them in new tactics and led them to a series of important victories. This army owed its loyalty to Marius rather than to the Senate or to Rome itself.

Marius tried to turn his popularity with his army and with the poor to political power in Rome. The general and his supporters badly frightened the Senate. The senators looked for a champion who would preserve their power. They found one in another general, Lucius Cornelius Sulla (SUL-uh), an aristocrat.

General Gaius Marius

Sulla had won many victories in Asia and Greece. But in 88 B.C. his enemies, mostly supporters of Marius, tried to have him removed from his command. Sulla refused the order and turned on Rome. He was the first Roman ever to attack his own city. Sulla drove out his enemies, killing as many as he could catch. He then marched off to continue the war in Greece. A short time later Sulla's enemies seized power in Rome once again and killed a large number of his supporters.

It was four years before Sulla could return to Rome, but he did so with a vengeance. He captured the city and ordered a mass slaughter of all those who had opposed him and many who had taken no part in politics at all.

Sulla revived the office of dictator. Now, no time limit was set on his powers. Yet Sulla lacked the ambition to be absolute ruler for long. He retired in 79 B.C. and died a little over a year later.

Sulla said he was restoring the power of the Senate. In the end, however, his career, like that of Marius, showed that the real power in Rome now rested with the army.

Lucius Cornelius Sulla

Julius Caesar

Among the many marked for death during Sulla's reign of terror was a talented and ambitious young man named Julius Caesar (SEE-zur). He was part of the anti-Senate group Sulla hated. Through a combination of luck and bribery Caesar was able to escape death. When Sulla pardoned him he is said to have grumbled that Caesar would ultimately do more harm to the Senate than anyone else.

Roman military power continued to expand throughout Europe and Asia, but in Rome itself there was chaos. No single group or individual could stay in power for long. Armed mobs supporting one or another political group roamed the streets, beating and often killing opponents. Politicians were friends one moment, deadly enemies the next.

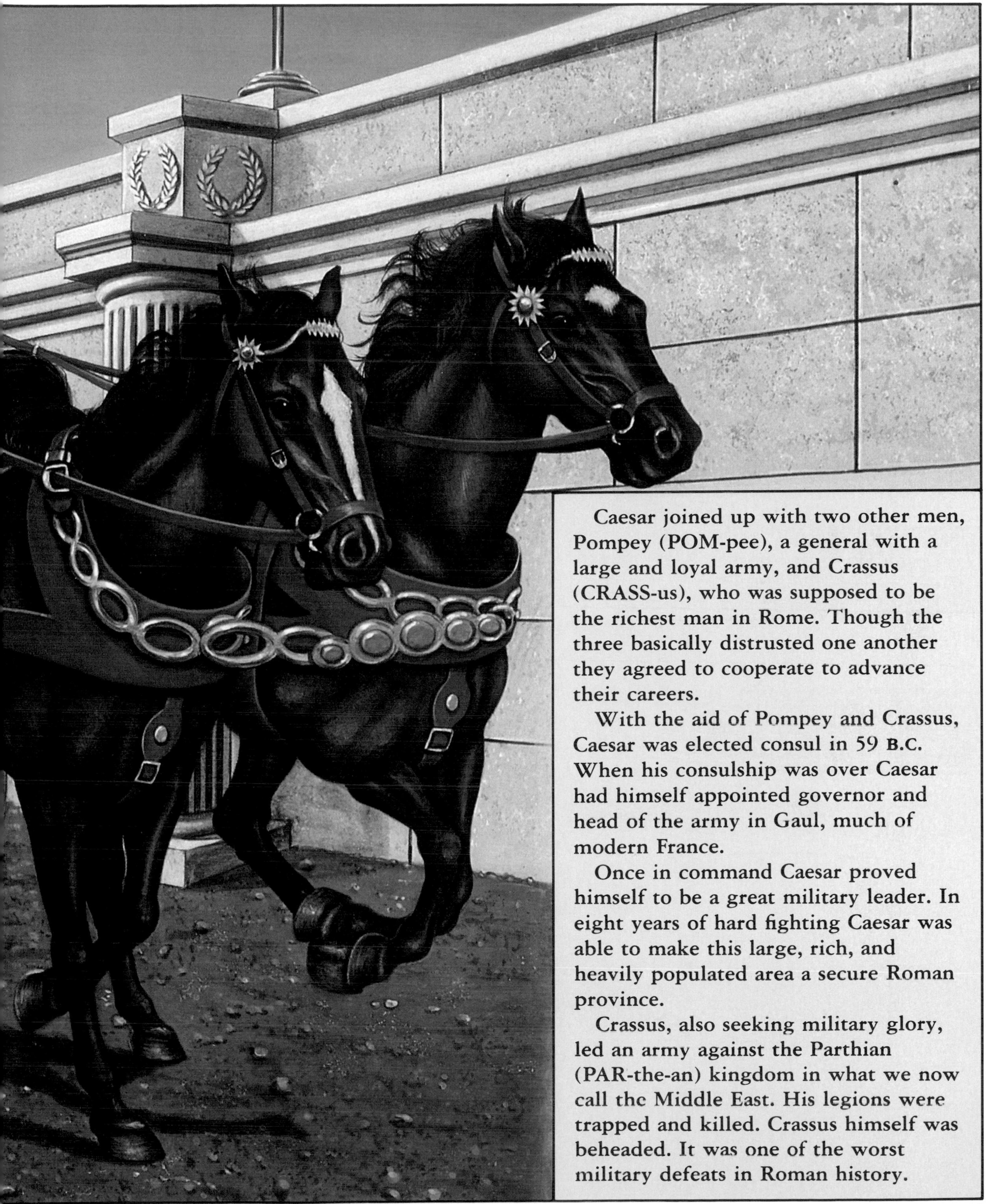

Caesar joined up with two other men, Pompey (POM-pee), a general with a large and loyal army, and Crassus (CRASS-us), who was supposed to be the richest man in Rome. Though the three basically distrusted one another they agreed to cooperate to advance their careers.

With the aid of Pompey and Crassus, Caesar was elected consul in 59 B.C. When his consulship was over Caesar had himself appointed governor and head of the army in Gaul, much of modern France.

Once in command Caesar proved himself to be a great military leader. In eight years of hard fighting Caesar was able to make this large, rich, and heavily populated area a secure Roman province.

Crassus, also seeking military glory, led an army against the Parthian (PAR-the-an) kingdom in what we now call the Middle East. His legions were trapped and killed. Crassus himself was beheaded. It was one of the worst military defeats in Roman history.

The End of the Republic

In Rome Pompey was won over by those members of the Senate who feared Caesar's growing power. Caesar was ordered to give up his command and return to Rome as a private citizen. Caesar knew that without his army behind him he would be killed. So on January 12, 49 B.C., Caesar and one of his legions crossed the little river Rubicon (RU-bi-con) and entered Italy. It was strictly against the law for him to do so, and yet another civil war began.

Within a few months Caesar had defeated Pompey's armies. Pompey himself fled to Egypt. The Egyptians had no taste for being on the losing side, so they killed him. Julius Caesar was now master of the entire Roman world.

With great energy Caesar tackled a huge number of problems. He had plans for everything from the debts that had built up during the civil wars to reforming the calendar. With small changes the Julian calendar, named after him, is still used today.

Those in the Senate who hated Caesar plotted against him. Caesar heard of threats to his life but was utterly fearless. On March 15, 44 B.C., he was surrounded by a group of plotters and stabbed to death.

The killers ran through the streets, shouting, "Liberty!" The result, however, was not liberty, but more civil war. Ultimately the victor was Octavian (ok-TAE-vi-an), a grandnephew of Julius Caesar, who had adopted him as his son and heir.

The First Emperor

Octavian was only eighteen when Caesar was murdered. For years he had to share power with some of Caesar's other associates, particularly Mark Anthony. Anthony married Octavian's sister but soon abandoned her for Queen Cleopatra of Egypt. Anthony spent most of his time in Egypt, while Octavian remained in Rome.

The shaky alliance between Octavian and Anthony lasted for some thirteen years, until Octavian felt secure enough to send a fleet to attack Anthony in Egypt. The attack was completely successful, and both Anthony and Cleopatra killed themselves rather than be taken back to Rome as prisoners.

Now there was a new master of the Roman world. He was a very different sort of person than Julius Caesar.

Caesar was bold. Octavian was cautious. Caesar was a great general who led his troops into battle and shared their dangers and hardships. Octavian was no soldier. He rarely even appeared on a battlefield. Yet Octavian

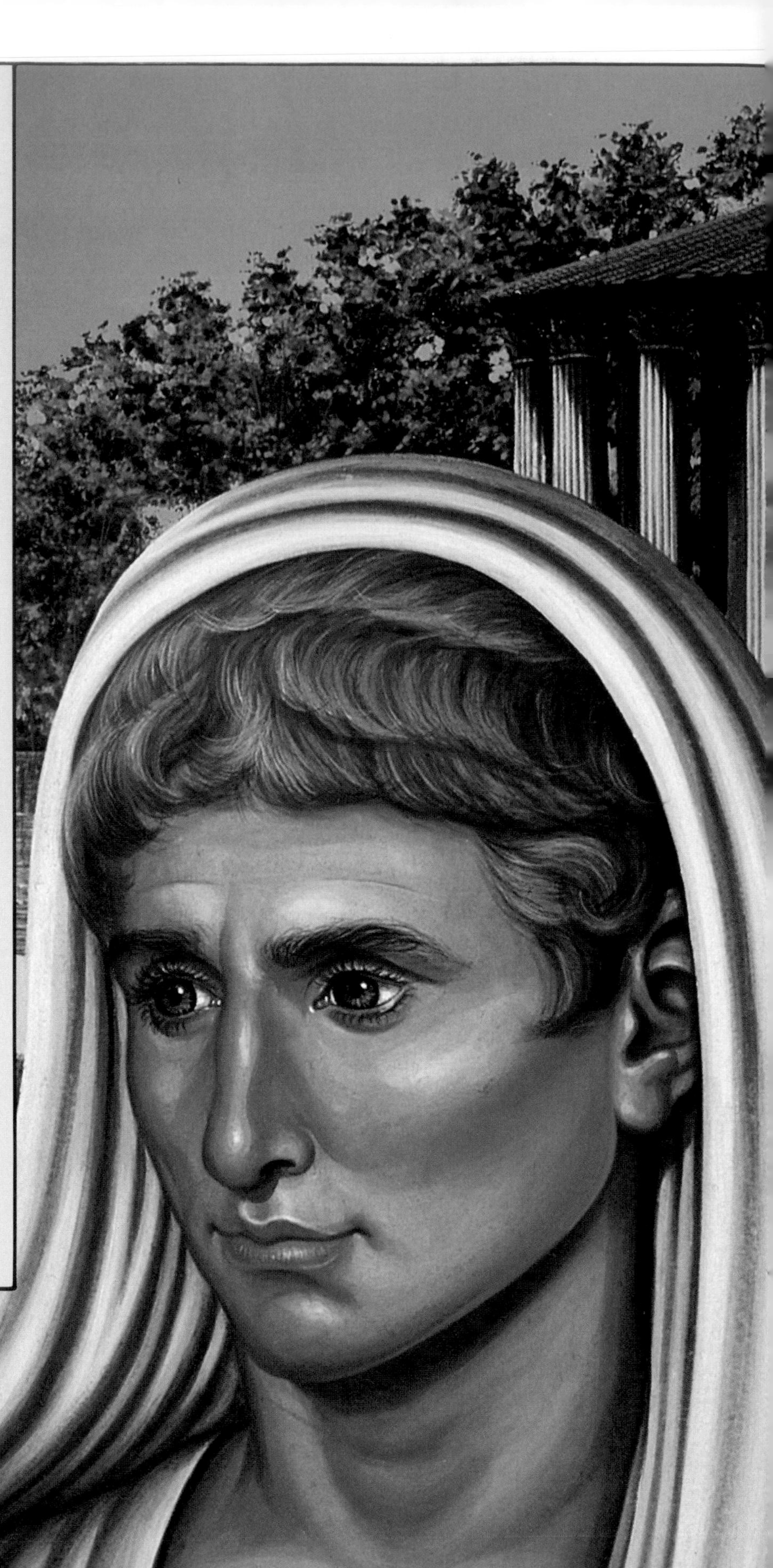

Augustus

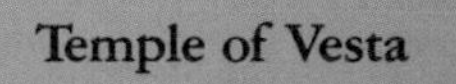
Temple of Vesta

understood Rome and the Romans better than Caesar had.

The Romans were tired of constant civil wars, and were ready for a strong ruler. Octavian, however, remembered what happened to Caesar. He did not wish to grab power openly. Slowly and patiently, he changed the nature of Rome from a republic to one-man rule. The Senate still met, but could do nothing unless Octavian approved. Still he always claimed to be following old republican traditions. He never called himself king or dictator. He took the name Augustus—which meant leader. Today we call him the emperor of Rome. At the time he was referred to as "first citizen."

Augustus had no desire for military glory. He stabilized the borders of the Empire, then reduced the size of the army. He tried to make the administration of Rome and the Empire as honest and efficient as possible. He changed the laws and the taxes. In effect, he changed just about everything, and practically everyone benefited. For artists, poets, and architects this was a Golden Age. Augustus gave the Roman Empire a period of peace and prosperity that it had never known before. And he set up a system of government that was to last for hundreds of years. When he died in A.D. 14 at the age of seventy-six, the Roman Senate and people declared him to be a god.

The Roman Soldier

During the late Republic and early Empire the Roman soldier was the best fighting man in the world.

He was armed with two metal-tipped *javelins,* or throwing spears. The spears had a fatal range of about ninety feet. For close combat he relied on a deadly two-foot-long sword.

Strapped to his left forearm was a large shield made of wood and bull's hide. The shield was strong enough to stop enemy sword thrusts and spears, as well as arrows and rocks.

The soldier's main item of clothing was a woolen tunic, covered by a leather vest, a heavy belt, and a short skirt made up of leather strips. On his feet he wore thick-soled sandals, studded with nails. His head was

protected by a bronze helmet.

In addition to his weapons the soldier carried a kettle and a food mill for grinding the staple of his diet, a cereal made of wheat. The Roman soldier didn't eat much meat.

Also in the soldier's baggage was a pickax, a saw, and other equipment for building a camp. While on the march a Roman army always built a well-defended place to sleep.

The discipline of the Roman soldier was famous. In battle he obeyed orders without question, and never retreated. Between battles soldiers quickly became restless, even rebellious. A good general had to inspire loyalty and respect among his troops. One way to do this was to bribe them with loot or high pay. But money was not enough. The general had to be able to communicate with his troops. Most of the great Roman generals were also great speakers. Julius Caesar said his ability to deliver stirring speeches was one of his most valuable assets.

Augustus

Caligula

Madmen and Showmen

The problem with one-man rule is that it works well enough if the leader has the talent and wisdom of Augustus. However, there was no guarantee that future leaders would be talented, wise, or for that matter even sane. Rome had both good emperors and bad ones.

Augustus was succeeded by his stepson Tiberius (tie-BEER-e-us), a gloomy, suspicious man but a good administrator. The weakness of the system really showed up with the next emperor, Caligula (Ca-LIG-u-la). He seemed a promising young man, but shortly after he took power he became very ill. That illness may have affected his mind. He had alarming swings in mood. When he was down, he felt everyone was plotting against him and he ordered many executions. When he was up, he thought he was a living god and wanted people to worship him. He was assassinated on the orders of the commander of the Praetorian (PRA-tor-i-an) Guard, the troops that

guarded the emperor. The commander thought Caligula was about to have him executed.

The next emperor was Caligula's uncle Claudius (CLAW-dee-us). He was lame, spoke with a bad stutter, and was thought to be feebleminded. He had never been considered as a possible emperor. After the murder of Caligula, the guardsmen found Claudius hiding behind some drapes and immediately hailed him as emperor. It turned out he was not a bad choice. Claudius had physical illnesses but there was nothing wrong with his mind. In fact, he wrote a number of books on Roman and Etruscan history.

Claudius was married four times and it was rumored that he was poisoned by his last wife so that her son Nero could become emperor. Nero became emperor when he was only sixteen. At the start he had good advisers and the government ran well. As Nero grew more self-willed, his weak and dangerous side showed up. He had both his wife and his mother murdered. He also lost any interest he might have had in actually running a government. He loved to perform, appearing on stage as an actor and singer. Nero also spent wildly and built a huge palace for himself.

As his unfitness to rule became more obvious the generals turned against him. Nero panicked and killed himself. His last words were, "What a showman the world is losing in me."

A Cruel Sport

For all their civilization, there was a streak of cruelty in the Romans. This showed most clearly in the horrifying shows where armed men called gladiators would fight one another, often to the death. Gladiatorial contests were first staged early in Roman history. They may have been introduced by the Etruscans. The contests remained very popular until the end of the Empire.

Gladiators were usually prisoners of war, slaves, or condemned criminals. Gladiatorial shows were held on public holidays and were often staged by emperors to boost their popularity. A Roman writer complained, "The people want only two things—bread and circuses." The bread was the free grain distributed to Roman citizens. The circuses were the gladiatorial shows.

The shows were held in open-air stadiums. Practically every Roman city had such a stadium. The largest and best known is the Colosseum in Rome itself. The Colosseum could hold about fifty thousand people.

In addition to the gladiatorial contests the Romans enjoyed other bloodthirsty shows. There were fights between different kinds of wild animals and contests between wild animals and men. Sometimes condemned criminals or members of persecuted groups like Christians were put in the arena with hungry lions or bears.

There were less gruesome events like chariot races. The most spectacular shows of all were the mock sea battles. The Colosseum could be flooded and turned into a miniature lake. Battles were fought between warships. Even this form of entertainment often resulted in injury and death.

Roman Women

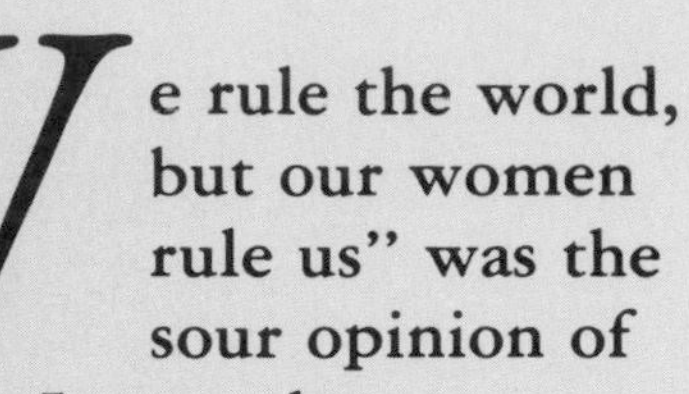

"We rule the world, but our women rule us" was the sour opinion of one Roman man. It was also an exaggeration, for from the farmer's family to the emperor's palace men held the power. Yet Roman women enjoyed greater freedom than those anywhere else in the ancient world. In Greece women had few rights. In Rome they could own wealth and land. They attended gladiatorial shows and, in fact, were some of the most enthusiastic fans of the games.

During the days of the Republic, women sometimes campaigned during elections—though they were not allowed to hold public office. Women could not speak before the Senate but they could make speeches in the Roman Forum, the chief gathering place for citizens.

The mothers and wives of emperors often played key roles in their careers. Nero thought his mother was too powerful, so he had her murdered.

One of the later emperors, Septimius Severus (sep-TIM-i-us se-VEER-us), who ruled from A.D. 193 to 211, was a strong-willed army man. However, his Syrian-born wife, Julia Domna, was equally strong-willed. She was often by his side during his campaigns, and helped plan his political strategy. She was called Mother of the Camp and the Senate and the Country. Julia also had a thirst for knowledge. She gathered around her a group of learned men including the Greek physician Galen, one of the great men in the history of medicine. Julia Domna earned the nickname "the philosopher."

A Roman Feast

The ordinary people of Rome ate simply. Their basic diet was bread, cereal, and vegetables. Occasionally they would eat fish, but very little meat.

The well-to-do Roman, on the other hand, might give a gigantic banquet. Even a simple dinner party began in midafternoon and lasted until well after dark.

During the meal, Romans lay on cushioned couches. They leaned on their left elbow while eating. They ate off silver plates and drank out of silver cups.

There were usually three courses. First came the appetizers—shellfish, lettuce, and eggs; then the main dishes —chicken and ham; and finally the dessert, fruit, and wine.

The feasts staged by some of the emperors were even bigger and have become famous. There were twenty or more courses featuring such strange foods as swans, sea urchins, and wild boar with truffles, a kind of mushroom. Nero, one of the most extravagant emperors, had a dining room where the ivory roof tiles could be pulled back to send down a shower of blossoms on the diners.

While the dinner could be pleasant the trip home might not be. At night Roman streets were dark and noisy. There was always the risk that someone on the roof of a tall building might empty a pot on your head.

The Roads of Rome

In order to keep their far-flung Empire together the Romans needed to move armies and administrators quickly from one place to another. That meant they needed good roads. The Romans were the best road builders of the ancient world. At the height of the Empire, Roman roads stretched from Scotland to the Persian Gulf and from North Africa to Central Asia.

Whenever possible Roman engineers laid out their roads in straight lines, over hills and through marshes. If a river stood in the way a bridge was built.

Roman roads were built to last. Many were still in use during the Middle Ages, long after the fall of the Empire. Some ancient Roman bridges are still being used.

In Italy and the more heavily populated provinces of the Empire there were milestones set up at every thousand paces along the road. These gave the distance to the nearest town and sometimes the distance between towns. There were regular guard stations and rest houses along every road. And eventually towns sprang up alongside the roads, with inns for weary travelers.

The Volcano

On August 24, A.D. 79, the volcano Mount Vesuvius (ve-SOO-vee-us) on the Bay of Naples erupted violently. Within a few terrible hours the Roman cities of Pompeii (pom-PAY) and Herculaneum (her-ku-LAI-ne-um) as well as several smaller villages were buried in ash and lava. Thousands of people died as a result of the catastrophe.

An eyewitness described how "on Mount Vesuvius broad sheets of fire and leaping flames blazed at several points, their bright glare emphasized by the darkness of the night."

While Pompeii and Herculaneum were buried, they were not totally destroyed. Sometimes the ash and mud preserved even the smallest and most fragile objects. At Herculaneum a lunch of bread, salad, cakes, and fruit was found on a dining room table.

Many of those who tried to run from the lava were not able to get away. In Pompeii the ash hardened around the bodies of the victims. When the bodies decomposed, hollow spaces or outlines of the bodies remained. Archaeologists (ar-ke-OL-o-jests) have poured plaster into these hollow spaces with astonishing results. The shape and the details of the body are reproduced down to the smallest detail. The shapes of animals—dogs, horses, and goats—were preserved in exactly the same way.

A Sense of Duty

No man was ever better prepared to be emperor than Marcus Aurelius (au-REE-li-us). He had been chosen as heir by Emperor Antoninus Pius (an-toe-NI-nus PIE-us). Marcus Aurelius was an intelligent, extremely hardworking man with a tremendous sense of duty. He was an example of the best sort of Roman.

In A.D. 161 Pius died and Aurelius took over. It was his bad luck to come to power at a time when the Empire was facing a new and very serious threat. The border of the Empire in Central Europe was the Danube (DAN-ube) River. On the other side lived German and other tribes. The Romans called them barbarians.

The barbarians began pouring across the Danube. Though they had always been a threat, these new attacks were

Marcus Aurelius

more serious and better organized than anything the Romans had seen before. Aurelius was forced to spend most of the final fourteen years of his life personally leading his army against the invaders. He was only partially successful. The German tribes were a problem for later emperors.

However, Marcus Aurelius is not best known as a ruler, but as a writer. Even in the midst of difficult military struggles, he wrote down his most personal thoughts. After his death, his writings were published in a book called *Meditations.* It is the most famous book ever written by a monarch.

Aurelius revealed himself as a man who found the burdens of ruling almost too much to bear. Yet he knew it was his duty to struggle on to the best of his ability. Life, he said, was a brief journey, and it is everyone's responsibility to behave as decently as we can to our fellow travelers.

"Men exist for each other," Aurelius wrote. "Then either improve them or put up with them."

Religion and the Empire

The official religion of Rome recognized many gods and was very formal. There were regular ceremonies and rituals for the gods that had to be performed. But there was no spiritual side to the religion. Priests were often political rather than religious figures. Julius Caesar was able to buy the position of chief priest of Rome and to use it to further his career.

In Rome religion and patriotism were closely tied. Many emperors were declared to be gods after they died. The emperors didn't necessarily take this too seriously. As one emperor was dying he said, "Oh dear, I fear I am becoming a god." But to worship at the temple of a divine emperor was a way of showing loyalty to the Empire itself.

There were many unofficial religions widely practiced in the Roman world. Some are called mystery religions because their rituals and rites were

Egyptian goddess Isis

supposed to be secret. The most widespread was the cult of the Egyptian goddess Isis. The mystery religions had very emotional ceremonies and gave worshipers a promise of life after death.

The Romans conquered people who practiced many different religions. So long as the conquered people observed the required rites of the official religion they were allowed to practice their own religion as well.

The Jews were a special problem. They fiercely believed in one God. For many Jews their religion made it impossible for them to perform the required ceremonies for the gods of Rome. There were a series of revolts in Jewish areas that were savagely put down by the Roman army.

Jesus was born during the reign of Augustus and crucified in the reign of Tiberius. At first the Romans regarded Christians as just another Jewish sect. As Christianity began to spread among non-Jews Roman authorities began to treat Christians differently. Sometimes Christians were tolerated, sometimes persecuted. It made little difference, for Christianity spread to all parts of the Roman Empire.

Constantine the Great

The emperor who came to be known as Constantine (CON-stan-teen) the Great reigned from A.D. 306 to 337. He changed the Roman Empire in two basic ways. First, he moved the capital from Rome, eastward to a city called Byzantium (by-ZANT-e-um). He renamed the city Constantinople in his own honor. The city is now the capital of modern Turkey and is called Istanbul (is-tan-BULL).

The second and even more far-reaching change was to convert the Empire to Christianity.

At first glance both of these changes look completely revolutionary. But they were not quite as unexpected as they appear. For many years emperors had spent relatively little time in Rome. From a military point of view it was not a good place for an emperor to control the vital frontiers. Byzantium on the Bosporus (BOS-por-res), a narrow body of water between Europe

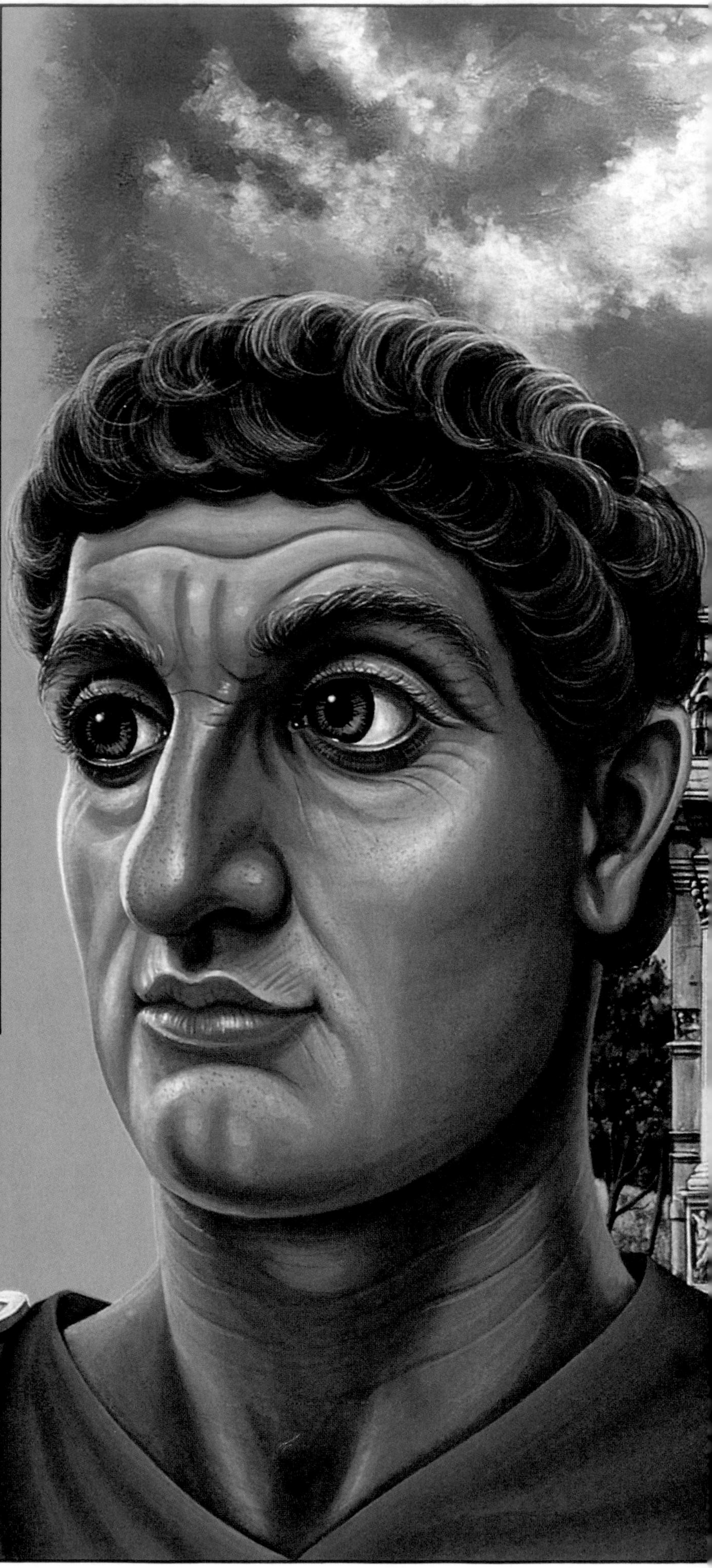

Constantine the Great and the Arch of Constantine

and Asia, was far better. It could also be defended by land and sea.

The switch to Christianity seems even more startling. Yet the old state religion of Rome with its many gods had long since lost its hold on people. There were a number of religions recognizing only a single all-powerful god that had attracted large followings throughout the Roman world. Some emperors had revered the Sun God. Constantine himself seems to have favored this religion at one time. So even before his switch to Christianity he had already become familiar with the idea of a single Supreme Being.

Some of Constantine's immediate predecessors had launched the most severe persecutions of Christians in history. But they failed to put an end to Christianity. The Christian communities remained strong and well organized. Constantine may have felt that the Christians were the only ones who could hold the Empire together.

While he probably had some political motives, there is no doubt that Constantine's Christianity was genuine. He insisted that before a crucial battle early in his career, he saw a vision of the cross in the sky.

Attila the Hun

In the years of its long decline the Roman Empire was attacked by a variety of barbarian peoples. None inspired as much terror as the Huns. And no barbarian leader has ever been as famous as Attila (a-TILL-uh).

The Huns were nomadic horsemen who originally came from Central Asia. They were small in number, but fierce fighters. The Romans first began to hear of the Huns in the year 376 when huge numbers of other barbarians fleeing the Huns begged permission to cross the Danube frontier and settle in Roman territory.

It wasn't until the following century that the Empire really felt the power of the Huns. In 445 Attila became king of the Huns in the usual way, by murdering his brother. He was more ambitious than other Hun leaders. In 447 the Huns poured across the Danube with such force that one Roman historian wrote, "Attila ground almost the whole of Europe into the dust."

A Roman ambassador who visited Attila's camp described the warlord this way:

"He was short of stature with a broad chest and a large head, his eyes small and sprinkled with grey; he had a flat nose and a swarthy complexion. . . . He was haughty in his walk, rolling his eyes hither and yon so that the power of his proud spirit appeared in the movement of his body."

In 452 Attila's armies were at the gates of Rome. A meeting was arranged between the king of the Huns and a delegation led by Pope Leo I. No one knows what was said at the meeting, but afterward Attila turned around and rode out of Italy.

Some said that Rome was saved by a miracle. Others suggested that Attila had been bribed. Still others, pointing out that disease had broken out in the Hun camp, believed that Attila wanted to keep the few men he had left.

The following year, Attila died suddenly. His many sons immediately began fighting with one another, and the Hun threat to the Roman Empire ended.

Fall of the West

The last emperor to rule a united Empire was Theodosius (the-o-DOH-shi-us) I. After his death in 395 the Empire was officially divided into eastern and western parts, each ruled by its own emperor. The senior emperor ruled from Constantinople. His junior colleague ruled from Rome.

The western emperors were weak, and most had brief reigns. Waves of barbarian invaders carved out their own kingdoms in Roman territory. In 410 Rome itself was actually captured briefly by Alaric (AL-a-rik), king of the Visigoths (VIS-a-goths). While the Visigoths occupied Rome for only three days, the event horrified the entire Roman world. Rome had not been occupied by a foreign foe in over eight hundred years. It was now clear that the western Roman Empire was falling apart.

Most historians say that the final fall came in 476. The emperor Romulus, who was only a boy and had reigned for less than a year, was forced from the throne by his own troops. All authority was transferred to Constantinople. The western Roman Empire, the heart of the old Roman Empire, ceased to exist.

It is strange that the last emperor at Rome and the legendary founder of Rome both had the same name—Romulus. There was also the legend that when Romulus founded Rome he looked for a sign in the sky. He saw twelve eagles. That meant that Rome would last 1,200 years. From 753 B.C. when Rome was said to have been founded to A.D. 476 is 1,229 years.

Charlemagne

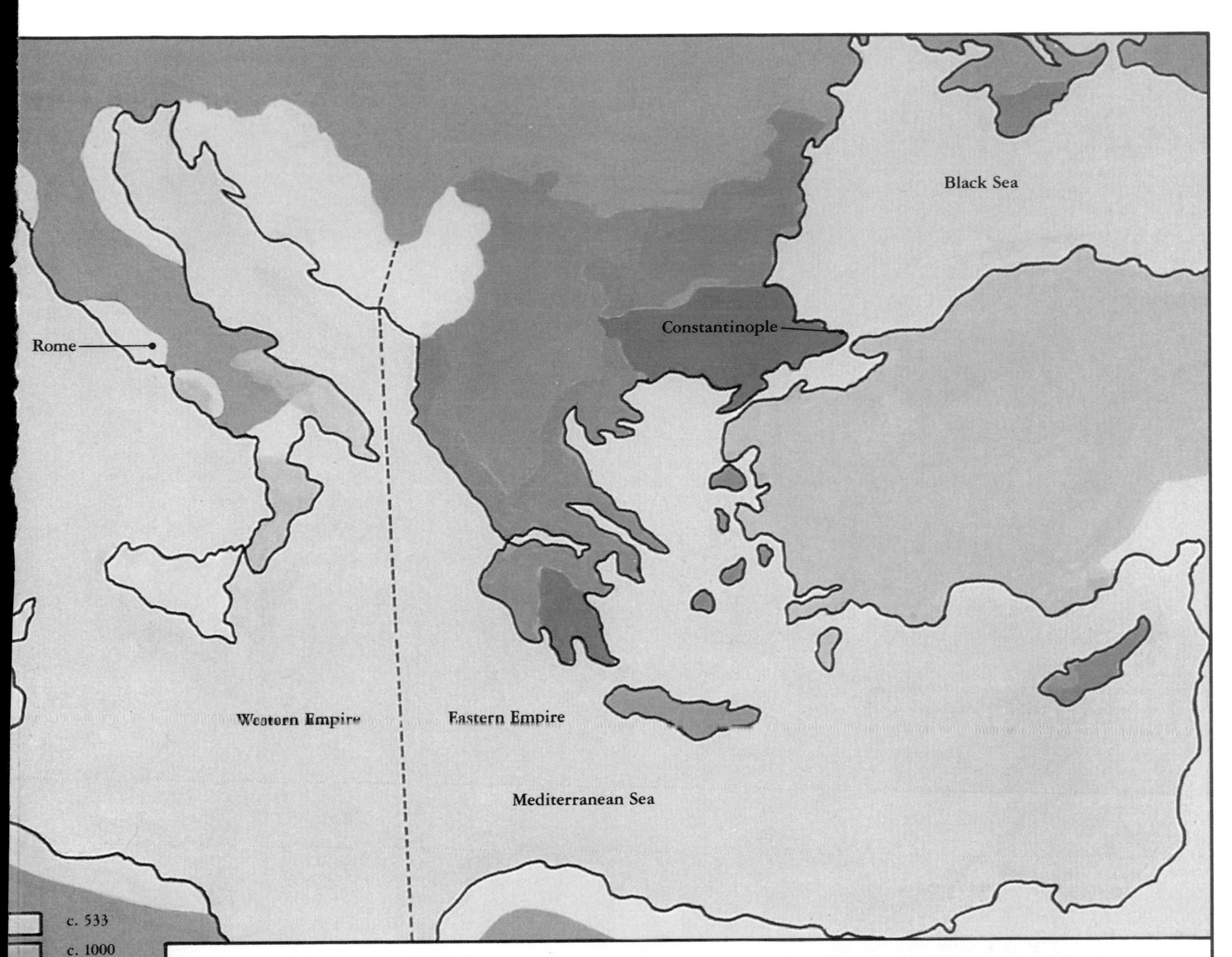

The Legacy of Rome

Only the western Roman Empire ended in 476. The center of power had long been in Constantinople. That city remained a world power for another thousand years. However, by this time the Empire is more properly called the Byzantine (byz-an-TEEN). There were attempts to reunite the entire Roman world, but they were short-lived.

Yet the idea of a universal Roman Empire hung on. In the year 800 Charlemagne (SHAR-le-main), king of a barbarian tribe called the Franks, was crowned Holy Roman Emperor. For centuries a combination of German states was called the Holy Roman Empire. The French conqueror Napoleon crowned himself emperor in imitation of the old Roman emperors in 1804.

Many of the languages of Europe, such as Italian, Spanish, and French, are called Romance languages because they are based on Latin, the language of the Roman Empire. Many words in the English language come from Latin.

Capitol Building, Washington, D.C.

Long after the end of the Roman Empire, Latin was still used by churchmen and scholars throughout Europe. It was the closest thing to a universal language that the Western world has ever known.

When the Founding Fathers of the United States were drawing up our Constitution, they looked back to the Roman Republic. Our legislative branch with its Senate and House of Representatives is based on the Senate and Assembly of the Roman Republic. Our nation is called a republic. Many of our Founding Fathers' ideas about the rights and duties of a citizen came from studying Roman history.

Our laws and languages, our architecture, engineering, and art, our religions, our calendar, and so much more were influenced by Rome.

The great Empire that began with a cluster of villages near the mouth of the Tiber River completely reshaped our world.

INDEX

Alaric, 42
Alps, 9, 15
Anthony, Mark, 22
Army, 13, 16–17, 19, 21, 23–25, 30, 32, 35, 38
Assembly, 12, 44
Attila, 40–41

Barbarians
- Germans, 34–35
- Huns, 40–41
- Visigoths, 42

Bosporus, 38
Byzantine Empire, 43

Caesar, Julius, 18–19, 21–23, 25, 36
Carthage, 14
Charlemagne, 43
Christians, 28, 37–39
Cincinnatus, 13, 16
Cleopatra, 22
Colosseum, 28
Constantinople (Byzantium, Istanbul), 38, 42–43
Consuls, 12, 19
Crassus, 19

Danube River, 34–35, 40
Dictator, 13, 17

Eastern Empire, 42
Egypt, 9, 21–22
Elephants, 15
Emperors
- Antoninus, Pius, 34
- Augustus (Octavian), 21–23, 26, 37
- Aurelius, Marcus, 34–35
- Caligula, 26–27
- Claudius, 27
- Constantine, 38–39, 42
- Nero, 27, 30–31
- Romulus, 42
- Severus, Septimius, 30
- Theodosius, 42
- Tiberius, 26, 37

Etruscans, 11–12, 28
Europe, 9, 18, 38, 40

Food, 25, 31, 33

Galen, 30
Gaul, 19
Gladiators, 28
Gods (Roman), 9, 23, 36
Greece, 9, 17, 30

Hannibal, 15
Herculaneum, 33
Holy Roman Empire, 43

Isis, 37
Italy, 9, 11, 14–15, 21, 32, 41

Jesus, 37
Jews, 37
Julia Domna, 30
Julian calendar, 21, 44

Latin, 43
Leo I (Pope), 41

Marius, Gaius, 16–17
Mars, 7
Meditations, 35
Mediterranean Sea, 9
Middle East, 9, 19
Mystery religions, 36–37

Napoleon, 43

Parthian kingdom, 19
Persia, 9
Pompeii, 33
Pompey, 19, 21
Praetorian Guard, 26–27

Remus, 7
Republic, 12, 21, 23–24, 30, 44
Roads, 32
Romance languages, 43
Romulus, 7, 42
Rubicon River, 21

Senate, 12–13, 16–18, 21, 23, 30, 44
Sulla, Lucius Cornelius, 16–18
Sun God, 39

Tiber River, 7, 9, 44
Turkey, 38

United States, 44

Vesuvius, Mount, 33

Weapons, 24–25
Western Empire, 42–43
Women, 30

About the Author

Daniel Cohen is a well-known author of nearly 150 books for young people—many of them on science, history, and the mysteries of the unknown. Several of his works have been cited as outstanding books for children by various organizations, including the Children's Book Council/National Science Teachers Association joint committee and the New York Public Library. He is the author of several other titles in Doubleday's line of nonfiction for younger readers—*Dinosaurs, Prehistoric Animals, Ancient Egypt, Ancient Greece*, and with his co-author and wife, Susan, *Zoos*.

The Cohens live in Port Jervis, New York.

About the Artist

Higgins Bond is an immensely talented young artist whose finely crafted illustrations have appeared in many forms—from books and magazines to calendars and collector's plates. She has also exhibited at several major museums, including the Metropolitan Museum of Art in New York.

Ms. Bond grew up in Little Rock, Arkansas, and later earned her bachelor's degree in fine arts from the Memphis (Tennessee) Academy of Arts.

The artist completed the paintings for *Ancient Rome* in acrylic after spending a great deal of time on research. "What's good about ancient Rome," she says, "is that there are lots of artifacts that show how the people looked. In using ancient sculpture as models for the characters, for example, I tried to imagine what these works of art would look like if they were not made of stone."

Ms. Bond currently lives in northern New Jersey with her husband and their fifteen-year-old son.

Pont du Gard in Nîmes, France